◀ NATIVE AMERICAN PEOPLE ▶

THE
HURON

by Craig A. Doherty and Katherine M. Doherty

Illustrated by Richard Smolinski

ROURKE PUBLICATIONS, INC.
VERO BEACH, FLORIDA 32964

CONTENTS

Printed in the USA

Library of Congress Cataloging-in-Publication Data

Doherty, Craig A.
   The Huron / by Craig A. Doherty, Katherine M. Doherty.
      p. cm. — (Native American people)
      Includes bibliographical references.
      1. Wyandot Indians—Juvenile literature.
   I. Doherty, Katherine M. II. Title. III. Series.
E99.H9D64 1994   973′.04975—dc20   93-32667
   ISBN 0-86625-528-1   CIP
                                                AC

Introduction

For many years archaeologists—and other people who study early Native American cultures—agreed that the first humans to live in the Americas arrived about 11,500 years ago. These first Americans were believed to have been big-game hunters who lived by hunting the woolly mammoths and giant bison that inhabited the Ice Age plains of the Americas. This widely accepted theory also asserted that these first Americans crossed a land bridge linking Siberia, in Asia, to Alaska. This land bridge occurred when the accumulation of water in Ice Age glaciers lowered the level of the world's oceans.

In recent years, many scientists have challenged this theory. Although most agree that many big-game hunting bands left similar artifacts all over the Americas 11,500 years ago, many now suggest that the first Americans may have arrived as far back as 20,000 or even 50,000 years ago. There are those who think that some of these earliest Americans may have even come to the Americas by boat, working their way down the west coast of North America and South America.

In support of this theory, scientists who study language or genetics (the study of the inherited similarities and differences found in living things) believe that there may have been more than one period of migration. They

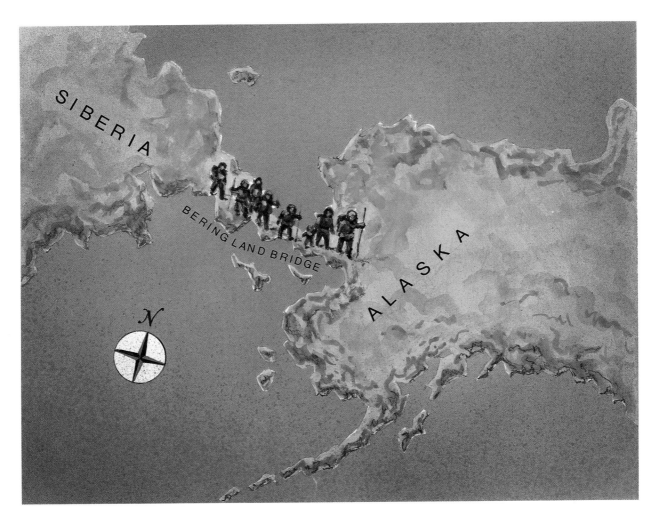

also believe that these multiple migrations started in different parts of Asia, which accounts for the genetic and language differences among the people of the Americas. Although it is still not certain when the first Americans arrived, scientists agree that today's Native Americans are descendants of early Asian immigrants.

Over the thousands of years between the first arrivals from Asia and the introduction of Europeans, the people who were living in the Americas flourished and inhabited every corner of the two continents. Native Americans lived above the Arctic Circle in the North to Tierra del Fuego at the tip of South America, and from the Atlantic Ocean in the East to the Pacific Ocean in the West.

During this time, the people of North America divided into hundreds of different groups. Each group adapted to the environment in which it lived. As agriculture developed and spread throughout the Americas, some people switched from being nomads to living in one area. Along the Mississippi River, in the Southwest, in Mexico, and in Peru, groups of Native Americans built large cities. In other areas, groups continued to exist as hunters and gatherers who had no permanent settlements.

A number of Native American groups that lived in the area from the eastern Great Lakes to the southern reaches of the Appalachian Mountains (also called the Eastern Woodlands) shared languages and culture. Archaeologists identify these groups as being part of the Iroquoian culture. The Iroquoian culture is in turn part of a larger group known as Woodland culture. The tribes that made up the Huron were part of this woodland cultural group.

Origins of the Huron

Archaeologists have determined that in the early stages of Iroquoian culture, bands of hunters and gatherers wandered throughout

the Eastern Woodlands. Approximately 1,000 years ago, agriculture reached this area and the people of the Iroquoian culture began to settle in agricultural communities. They kept cultural similarities, but developed distinct tribal differences. Tribes formed their own languages and customs.

The Huron were a group of five tribes of the Iroquoian cultural group. They lived at the eastern end of Georgian Bay on Lake Huron in a small area that extended east to Lake Simcoe in what is now Ontario Province, Canada. Huron was the name given to these people by the early French explorers. In French, the word Huron means "boar," but it also means "ruffian" or "savage," which is how some historians assume the French explorers meant it. The people whom the French called the Huron called themselves the Wendat, which means "island" or "peninsula people," referring to their geographic location, which was almost surrounded by water.

Just prior to the arrival of the French in Huron territory, between 20,000 and 30,000 Huron lived in twenty-five villages. Their largest villages had populations of about 2,000 people each. The area they lived in, called Huronia, was approximately thirty-five to forty miles east to west and twenty miles north to south.

Daily Life

The primary structure of the Huron was the longhouse, called *ganonchia* in the Wendat language. The typical longhouse was fifteen to twenty feet wide and up to one hundred feet long. To build a longhouse, a frame was first erected using wooden poles from a variety of trees. The pole frame was then covered with bark. Cedar bark was preferred. One drawback to using cedar bark was that it burned easily and quickly if it caught fire.

Longhouses were separated from each other and were built with one end facing the prevailing wind. That way, if one burned, the fire would not spread as easily to the others of the village. Archaeologists believe that fire would cause longhouse inhabitants to suffer a major loss of property as well as lives, since the Huron often buried their valuables inside the longhouse or nearby, for safekeeping.

Inside every longhouse there were several hearths about twenty feet apart. Each hearth was shared by two nuclear families that were part of an extended family that inhabited the whole longhouse. A nuclear family has a mother, a father, and their children. An extended family is made up of grandparents, aunts, uncles, and their children. One nuclear family lived on either side of the hearth. Down both sides of the longhouse ran a platform raised four to five feet off of the ground. These platforms were used as both work areas and sleeping areas.

Cooking utensils and other belongings were hung from the ceiling, and food was stored under the platforms. Reed mats covered the platforms and also served as doors into the longhouse. In the winter, fur blankets were added to the beds for warmth.

Early French explorers, traders, and missionaries were amazed at how so many people could live in such close

Longhouses were built slightly apart from one another.

quarters with little or no privacy. One drawback to the longhouse, which the Huron shared with their domesticated dogs, was the vermin that often infested them. Mice and rats were also a problem, as were fleas and lice.

Larger villages also had two bigger longhouses that were not used as residences. These were the houses of the civil chief and the war chief of the village. They were up to 180 feet long and were mainly used for ceremonial purposes. Community meetings were held in the civil chief's house.

The Huron built their villages on the tops of hills and surrounded them with a palisade, or a wall made of upright logs buried closely together to form a fence. The logs were usually sharpened on the exposed end. The purpose of the palisade was to protect the inhabitants from any other tribes that might raid their village. Unlike some Iroquoian tribes, the Huron built their villages within a mile or two of the next village. This way, the villages could aid in each others' defense and help to strengthen the bonds between them.

Family Life

The family played an important role in the lives of the Huron. A matriarchal family structure prevailed, meaning

that when a couple married they lived with the wife's extended family. Longhouses were usually occupied by a group of sisters, their mother and father, their husbands, and their children. The children became members of the mothers' clan.

Marriage and courtship among the Huron involved the families of an intended couple agreeing to a marriage. A man's family often gave him presents to offer a woman. They would also approach her family to see if such a marriage suited them. If a woman accepted the gifts, it was assumed that she was interested in the young man. After a period of courtship, a woman's father hosted a feast for the two families and their friends. At the feast, the father of the bride would announce the intentions of the couple to be husband and wife. After the announcement was made by the father, the couple was considered married.

Raising children was a community responsibility. Everyone took part in helping teach the children skills they would need to help the family and the tribe survive. Infants were bound to cradle boards, which were a couple of feet long and about a foot wide. Some cradle boards were beautifully decorated with painted designs and beads. Babies were bound to their cradle boards with furs, and seemed content to observe the world quietly.

A Huron mother kept her baby on a cradle board with her as she worked

A young Huron man offers gifts as part of his courtship.

8

on the tasks involved in feeding her family. The mother would hang the cradle board up with the baby on it so the child could see her as she worked. If she had to travel somewhere, she would take the baby on its cradle board with her, wrapped in the front of her dress so the baby could look at her. If the mother had to travel a longer distance, she would carry the cradle board on her back and use a tumpline. A tumpline is a strap that goes from a pack, basket, or cradle board around the forehead of the carrier.

When children were able to, they began to help with the daily tasks of the family. Among the Huron there was a strong division of labor between males and females. Girls were taught the skills of their mothers, who were primarily responsible for preparing food. The care of the Huron fields was given to the women, although the men often helped during the busiest times of planting and harvesting. The women also showed the young girls which plants they should gather from the forest and how to preserve them for the winter.

Boys were encouraged to practice the skills that would make them excellent hunters and warriors. At an early age, boys were given a bow and spent countless hours practicing, trying to hunt small game near the village when they could. Boys also helped the men in building longhouses, clearing the fields, building canoes, and other tasks that were important to the welfare of the family and village.

Instead of formal schooling, both boys and girls learned by watching the adults and listening to them tell stories as they worked. Children learned all about the history of their tribe and the important religious and moral lessons of the community. Storytelling was also an important way to pass time during the worst of the winter weather. Early French observers of the Huron were amazed that the adults never seemed to punish their children.

Huron women taught their daughters how to plant and harvest food.

Food Growing and Gathering

Providing food for both the family and village was the most important and time-consuming activity for all members of the Huron tribe. Corn was the staple item in the Huron diet and required the greatest amount of work. The Huron planted their corn repeatedly in the same fields surrounding their villages. Every ten to twenty years, the soil became depleted and new fields needed to be cleared. There were times, when all the available land near the village site had been used up, that entire Huron villages moved to a new location that offered fresh, uncleared land.

Clearing the land was very difficult. Stone axes were used to cut brush and smaller trees. Larger trees had their bark stripped off all the way around the trunk. This technique would kill the tree. After the tree was dead, the Huron would build a fire around its base. As the tree slowly burned, the Huron would chip away the blackened wood with their axes. Eventually, the

*Huron men clear the land
to create fields for planting.*

tree would be burned all the way through and fall to the ground.

In the first few years of a new field, the yield of corn was usually high. Corn was stored in large wooden containers in a corner of the longhouse. The Huron also grew beans and squash.

Although in ancient times the Huron had existed entirely on wild foods, gathering food eventually became a less important task. Wild berries—raspberries, blackberries, strawberries, and blueberries—were the major crops of the Huron. A large share of the berries were eaten fresh, and the remainder was dried for future use in winter soups and cakes.

11

Young boys practice their skills with bows and arrows.

Hunting and Fishing

While the women worked in the fields, the men were busy providing for the needs of the family and the village. Hunting and fishing were important sources of food and other materials. The Huron people ate more fish than they did meat.

Living in an area of abundant lakes and ponds allowed the Huron people to become excellent fishermen. Their most important fishing time was in the fall, when large numbers of whitefish and other species would move into the shallows of Georgian Bay to feed. While the fish were in the shallows, the Huron could easily spear them. A Huron fish spear was carved from wood and had three barbed points at the end of its shaft.

During this time, many Huron moved to fishing camps that were on islands in the bay. They often stayed as long as a month, catching and processing fish. If the weather was warm and dry, the fish were cleaned and then laid out on wooden racks to dry. If the weather was too damp for drying, the fish were then smoked. Later the fish were packed in bark containers for transport back to the mainland villages. Some whitefish were boiled to extract the oil for use in cooking.

Huron hunters use a weir to trap fish in order to spear them.

13

Geese were often trapped in nets by Huron hunters.

Besides spearing, the Huron used many other tactics to catch fish. Weirs were used in streams and narrows where fish were plentiful. A weir is a series of man-made obstructions that force fish to pass through a narrow opening. As the fish pass through this narrow funnel in the weir, they can be quickly speared or netted.

The Huron were also known to have fished using a line and hook. In the winter they often fished through holes they cut in the ice. One ice-fishing method involved cutting several holes around a large circle on the surface of the ice. Once these holes were cut, the Huron were able to string a net from hole to hole and then lower it into the water. When the net was hauled back

up, many fish would be caught in it. Fish were often eaten fresh, although dried fish was an important ingredient in the corn soups and stews that were the tribe's main staples. Meat was also a component of the Huron diet.

Hunting was an important activity for the Huron man, but because so many Huron lived in a relatively small area, game was scarce close to the villages. To the east of their territory, along the north shore of Lake Ontario, was an area that was uninhabited. These were the Huron hunting grounds, which abounded in wildlife.

Deer, bear, beaver, and other small mammals were all hunted, as were many types of wild birds. The larger mammals were more important to the

14

Huron for their skins than they were
for their meat.

Deer were hunted in a variety of
ways. Sometimes the Huron, like
other Woodland tribes, would build
two long fences in the woods that
came together at one end like a funnel.
Over a period of a few days, the Huron
hunters would drive deer into the wide
end of the funnel. When the deer
reached the narrow end, other hunters
would be waiting to shoot them with
their bows. Over one hundred deer
might be harvested during a month-
long fall hunting trip. Although some
meat was eaten, the main objective was
to get deerskins for making clothes.
Hunting trips often lasted until there
was snow on the ground. The snow

helped the hunters, as it allowed them
to bring the hides back on sleds.

The Huron hunted bears by using
dogs to chase them up into trees.
Once a bear was in a tree, the hunters
could shoot it with their bows. Beavers
were also hunted by the Huron. During
the winter, beavers stay in their lodges.
The Huron would break through the
top of the lodges and kill the beavers
inside. Beaver meat was eaten and the
furs used for clothing.

Some Huron hunters shot birds with
their bows, although the preferred
method of catching birds was to net
them. In the fall, large flocks of geese
and ducks would land in Huron fields,
where hunters would net them as the
birds fed on the ripening corn.

Food Preparation

Corn, the primary food in the Huron diet, was prepared in many different ways. The most common form it took was as corn soup, the ingredients of which varied depending on what was available. Fish or meat might be added, as would berries and other plant foods. Ashes were often thrown in to give the soup more flavor. Corn was also roasted when it was fresh, along with slices of squash.

The Huron made cornbread as well. To create the flour, corn was ground between two stones. In another method, dried corn kernels placed in a hollowed-out upright log were pounded with a pole up to eight feet long. Berries, either fresh or dried, depending on the time of year, were often added to the bread, which was then baked buried within the ashes of the fire.

The Huron usually ate twice a day, once in the morning and again in the evening. The cooking fires of the Huron were kept going almost all of the time. If the fire went out, coals from a neighboring hearth could be used to relight the fire. The Huron also knew how to light a fire using the friction of two sticks and some very dry tinder.

Clothing

Huron clothes were typical of those of the Woodland tribes of the time. Both men and women wore breechcloths made of deerskin. The women often

A Huron woman makes a loaf of cornbread, a staple food in the tribe's diet.

wore skirts over their breechcloths. Both men and women were bare above the waist during the warmer months. They often covered their bare skin with oil or animal fat for protection from the sun and wind. Sometimes they mixed colors with the oil or fat and decorated their bodies with pictures or designs. In the winter, fur shirts and robes were added to these outfits for warmth, as were deerskin leggings that went from the ankle to high upon the thigh.

Both men and women wore moccasins, usually made of deerskin. The importance of animal skins in the Huron wardrobe made the skins quite valuable. Long before the French

A man and woman dressed in the traditional clothing of the Huron.

17

began trading with Native Americans for furs, the Huron had an extensive trade network with their Algonquian neighbors to the north and east. The Huron traded their surplus corn for these skins.

Travel

Whether they were traveling to hunt, fish, or trade, the Huron ranged over a large territory outside the area of their villages. They traveled a wide network of trails on foot. Foot trails tended to

The Huron built finely crafted birchbark canoes in which to travel throughout wide areas.

follow the high ground, where the woods were usually less dense and the ground was drier. In the winter they traveled on snowshoes, an invention of the early Woodland tribes. When the lakes and rivers of the area were free of ice, the Huron traveled by canoe.

The Huron built birchbark canoes, which were superior to the canoes of other tribes that did not have the right kind of birch growing in their area. The Huron canoes came in a variety of sizes. The largest were approximately twenty feet long and could carry six men. Smaller canoes were also built as they could easily be carried over the many routes between the lakes and rivers of the area.

Birchbark canoes were light and easy to paddle, but they were also quite fragile and often leaked. When traveling by canoe, the Huron stayed close to shore, where they could beach their canoes if there was a problem. Early French explorers and traders who first entered the area traveled by boat and used many ports created by the Huron and other local Native Americans.

Games

Although life among the Huron was not easy and required everyone to do a lot of work, there was still time for play. Children often played games that mimicked the roles they would have as adults. The Huron also had many other kinds of games. One, called *aescara*, required 300 to 400 white reeds, each about 12 inches long. Although we now know that this was played by the Huron, the rules of this game are unknown in modern times.

One popular Huron and Woodland tribal game that most people are familiar with is lacrosse. Young Huron men played this game with a hard ball and sticks. The Huron lacrosse sticks, long wooden sticks hooked at one end, were not very different from those used today. Netting was attached to the end with a hook, and a ball was caught, carried, and thrown with the netting. The object of lacrosse was to get the ball into the other team's goal.

The Huron also played a game that used a dish and a number of fruit pits or pottery pieces. In either case, one side of each marker was painted white and the other black. The object was to bang the dish on the ground so that all the markers tumbled inside it and ended up on the same-color side. Whatever the game being played, it is thought that the Huron liked to gamble on the outcome. Sometimes personal items such as clothes were wagered.

Political and Social Organization

Among the Huron people there were several different levels of political and social organization. Socially, the family was the most important structure.

Opposite: The game of lacrosse was extremely popular with young Huron men. Above: Huron Chief White Eagle, at sixty years old.

Extended families cooperated to provide food, shelter, and clothing for their members.

In addition to belonging to a family, every Huron belonged to one of eight clans: Bear, Beaver, Deer, Hawk, Porcupine, Snake, Turtle, or Wolf. A clan is a group of people who are believed to have descended from common ancestors. Among the Huron it

21

was believed that each clan was descended from one of either original Huron mothers. Children were considered members of their mother's clan. When it came time for Huron children to marry, they were expected to choose someone from a clan other than their own or their father's. Representatives of each clan were found in almost all Huron villages and were the same among the five different Huron tribes.

The primary political unit of the Huron was the village. In many ways, each village functioned on its own. Within the village, each clan had its own chief, who looked out for the interests of the members of the clan. The chiefs of the clans would meet to form a village council and make decisions that affected the whole village. Unlike the government we have today, the Huron village chiefs had no way of forcing people to do what they said. Therefore, it was important that the chiefs made decisions with which most of the people agreed. To do this, the council of chiefs often consulted the older members of the community before a decision was made. Among the Huron, the older members of the community were greatly respected for their knowledge and wisdom. The position of chief was a hereditary one, passed down from one chief to another member of his clan and his family. Since a man's children belonged to the clan of his wife, the position of chief would be passed to one of the chief's sister's sons.

Each village also belonged to a confederation that connected all of the Huron people together into one political unit. The confederation was similar to what we call a country today. The five tribes were similar to states within that country, and the villages were the cities and towns that make up the state. The Huron confederation was overseen by a council of chiefs. Each village would send one or more of their village chiefs to a council each spring. The village that hosted the council would be responsible for feeding and entertaining the visiting chiefs. In return, the visiting chiefs would bring gifts for their hosts.

The confederation council of chiefs dealt with problems that affected the whole group. Those issues might include disputes between villages or relations with other tribes. The spring council of chiefs might last as long as three weeks. Each session of the council began with the ceremonial smoking of pipes. Tobacco was a sacred plant to many Native American groups. The Huron believed that the smoke gave them the ability to think more clearly about the problems they faced. The council of chiefs, like the village chiefs, had no way of forcing their decisions on the people, and so they had to create solutions that would please almost everyone.

Early French visitors to the Huron were amazed that the council could rule over thousands of people without a single police officer. Although they did not have a police force, the Huron did have the equivalent of an army.

One of the most important duties of a Huron man was to be a warrior, and every village had, besides its clan chiefs, a war chief. This war chief probably did not inherit his position, but was most likely selected because of his intelligence and his demonstrated prowess as a warrior. Although the

Huron lived in harmony among themselves, their relations with neighboring tribes were not always as tranquil. They especially had problems with the Iroquois who lived south of Lake Ontario in what is today the state of New York.

Most problems with other tribes arose over territorial disputes. Although the Huron lived in a relatively small area, they claimed a vast territory as their hunting grounds. Besides disputes over hunting territory, there were also trade relations with other tribes that had to be protected. Finally, war was important to many Native Americans as a way for a man to achieve status and respect within his own group. For many, the Huron included, warfare with other tribes was an accepted part of life.

Religious Life

The Huron, like other members of the Iroquoian culture, believed that the earth was created at a time when the Sky Woman, called *Aataentsic,* fell toward the oceans that covered the earth. To give her a place to land, the animals dove to the bottom of the sea and brought up mud, which was then piled on the back of a giant turtle. *Aataentsic* landed right on the turtle's back, which became the lands of the people. Once on earth she gave birth to twin boys, called *Tawiscaron* and *Iouskeha.*

A Huron warrior swings his tomahawk in a demonstration of strength.

In the Huron creation myth, Aataentsic, the Sky Woman, fell toward the earth and landed on the back of a giant turtle.

The twins were believed to have lived as the Huron did, in a longhouse that was surrounded by fields. The twins' homeland was the village of the dead where the souls of the Huron went to live, believed to be somewhere toward the west of the Huron territory. The sun always went to this village of the dead at the end of each day.

The Huron believed that *Iouskeha* was the good twin, responsible for all the good things that happened. His brother, *Tawiscaron,* was the bad twin.

He and his mother, *Aataentsic,* were thought to spend their time trying to undo the good that *Iouskeha* did. The Huron believed that *Iouskeha* was responsible for liberating all the animals from a cave where they had been living. As the animals left the cave, he wounded each in one leg so that it would be easier for the Huron to successfully hunt them. Legends say that he missed the wolf as it left the cave, and so it was always the hardest animal for the Huron to hunt.

*A **shaman** invokes the spirits in an attempt to cure an ill Huron man.*

26

Huron burial platforms are raised almost ten feet above the ground.

Besides families, clans, villages, and tribes, many Huron belonged to one of at least four religious societies. One of these, the *Atirenda,* taught its members how to cure people.

The leaders of the religious aspect of Huron life were called *shamans.* These men were knowledgeable in the religious ceremonies and obligations of the Huron. They were similar to modern-day priests, ministers, or rabbis.

When a Huron became sick, he or she believed that the cause came from the spirit world. The process of curing a sick Huron would thus often involve feasts and dances to appease the spirits. The Huron also had knowledge of the medicinal plants and roots that could help cure illnesses.

The remaining religious societies were responsible for other aspects of the spiritual life of the village and tribe. One of the most important of these was preparing the dead for their trip to the spirit world. The spirits of all living creatures were treated with respect. The Huron would never burn the bones of a fish or an animal that they had eaten.

The proper burial of a dead member of the community required much preparation. A feast was given in his or her honor, and the deceased's most valuable possessions were buried as well. Because it was believed that the dead would live much as they had in this world, their tools and food were often placed in the grave. A Huron was either buried in the ground with stakes surrounding the grave to mark the spot, or raised on a platform that was eight to ten feet tall.

It was believed that some spirits did not make it to the village of the dead and would remain among the living. These spirits were often thought to be the cause of illnesses and other problems among the Huron.

European Contact

For the Huron tribes of Ontario, contact with Europeans quickly led to the destruction of a way of life that had taken thousands of years to develop. In 1609, a group of Huron warriors met Samuel de Champlain on the St. Lawrence River. Champlain, an explorer and map maker, was the leader of French efforts to establish the colony of New France in what is now Canada. Five years later, in 1614, Champlain was the first European to visit the homelands of the Huron. He spent about five months among them.

The Huron were already established traders in the region, and Champlain and other French fur traders saw them as an important link in forming their new colony. The French treated the Huron well and used them as intermediaries in the fur trade. At first, the Huron prospered in this role.

To the south, however, their long-time rivals, the Iroquois, were trading with the British colonies. The British supplied the Iroquois with guns and encouraged them to use the guns against the French, as well as their Native American allies. In addition, the demands of the fur trade reduced the numbers of beavers and other animals whose furs were valuable, causing many Native Americans to travel outside of their traditional hunting grounds in search of pelts. This increased the problems between the Iroquois and the Huron.

Depletion of the fur-bearing animals and increased hostilities with the Iroquois caused many problems for the Huron in the first years of European contact. However, the greatest problem came unseen and unannounced. Between 1634 and 1640, a series of terrible epidemics spread through the Huron communities. Native Americans throughout North America lacked immunities to diseases unwittingly introduced by Europeans. Smallpox, measles, and other diseases had devastating effects on the Huron.

Although early estimates set the population as high as 30,000 to 40,000 Huron, scientists today believe that the pre-epidemic Huron population was between 18,000 and 22,000 people. By 1640, only 9,000 Huron remained. The weakened survivors tried to continue with their lives.

During the 1640s, the Iroquois nearly finished off the Huron. Attacks of increasing savagery continued during this time, and by 1649 the Huron culture was all but wiped out. The Huron people whom the Iroquois had not killed or taken captive split in two. Some went east, where they settled in the protective shadow of Quebec City.

Mary McKee, a Huron woman in Ontario, Canada, with traditional grinding tools.

The Huron meet Samuel de Champlain.

Others went west and merged with different people of the area.

The eastern branch of the Huron, although frequently forced to relocate, remained in the Quebec area. These Huron intermarried with French settlers and increasingly lost their cultural identity. The land they were allowed to settle was poor in comparison with their homelands, and they soon gave up farming for hunting, trapping, and making crafts. Eventually, many of the Huron were assimilated into the mainstream culture of Quebec.

The western branch of the remaining Huron is harder to track. They joined with the survivors of the Tionontati tribe and moved westward. About 800 members comprised this combined tribe, which became known as the Wyandot. The Wyandots were pushed around the upper Midwest as the frontier continually expanded west. The last of the Wyandots now live in the state of Oklahoma.

Annie Edmons and Tina Faber play with their dolls at the Wyandotte reservation in 1882.

Miss Boone's school, at a Huron reservation in Oklahoma.

The Huron Today

The Huron of Canada lost almost all tribal identity when their lands in Quebec were sold or taken by the government and they were left with about 26 acres. In 1968, the Huron lands were increased to over 165 acres. This reserve, called Wendake, now has approximately 1,000 people living on it. Two manufacturing facilities at Wendake produce about 50,000 pairs of snowshoes and 3,000 canoes a year. About 1,000 other Huron people live elsewhere in Canada and in the United States.

As for the Wyandots, about 500 still live on the Wyandotte reservation in Oklahoma. Another group lives in Sandwich, Ontario, near their ancestral homelands. In addition, 1,500 people in the United States and Canada identify themselves as Wyandots.

None of the surviving Wyandots or Huron speak their original Iroquoian language. Most of their customs have been lost. There is, however, an increasing awareness among these people of their shared history and unique identity as Native Americans.

Chronology

1609   Huron warriors meet Samuel de Champlain, French explorer.

1614   Champlain is the first European to visit the homelands of the Huron; he lives with them for five months.

1626   Jesuit priests are the first Europeans to visit the Huron.

1634–1640   A series of epidemics kills over half of the Huron population.

1640s   Ongoing warfare with the English-supported Iroquois.

1647   Huron subgroup, called the Arendaronon, are wiped out by warfare.

1648   Huron villages of Teanaustaye and Saint Ignace are abandoned.

1649   Huron people are totally defeated by the Iroquois. Those Huron not taken captive or killed are split into two groups: One resettles near Quebec; the other becomes the Wyandots and frequently moves around the American frontier before eventually settling in Oklahoma.

1671   Peace settlement between the Iroquois and the Wyandots.

1697   The Huron who settled in Quebec move to Lorette, outside Quebec City, where some remain today. Their reserve is officially called the Village-des-Hurons.

1728   Some Wyandots settle near Detroit, Michigan.

1842–1843   As part of the Removal Act of 1830, Wyandots in Ohio and Michigan are forced to trade their lands for property in Kansas.

1855   A treaty is signed that gives the Wyandots full status as American citizens but eliminates their tribe. After this, some of the Wyandots move to Oklahoma.

1968   Huron land is increased from about 26 acres to over 165 acres.

INDEX

Acknowledgments and Photo Credits
Cover and all artwork: Richard Smolinski.
P. 21: Canadian Museum of Civilization, Negative #96030; p. 28: Canadian Museum of Civilization,
Negative #19946; p. 30: Canadian Museum of Civilization, Negative #18255 (top), Smithsonian
Institution/National Anthropological Archives (bottom).
Map by Blackbirch Graphics, Inc.